Editorial Project Manager

Lorin E. Klistoff, M.A.

Illustrators

Sue Fullam

Janice Kubo

Cover Artist

Brenda DiAntonis

Art Manager

Kevin Barnes

Art Director

CJae Froshay

Imaging

James Edward Grace

Publisher

Mary D. Smith, M.S. Ed.

Bible Story Activities

Ten Commandments

Author

Mary Tucker

Teacher Created Resources, Inc.

12621 Western Avenue

Garden Grove, CA 92841

www.teachercreated.com

ISBN: 978-1-4206-7050-9

©2005 Teacher Created Resources, Inc.

Reprinted, 2016

Made in U.S.A.

Ten Commandments

Introduction

Recently, a polling group asked Americans questions about the Bible. Of those who called themselves Bible-believing Christians, a huge percentage could not name the Ten Commandments! The percentage should be much lower among children who have studied the Old Testament in Sunday school. However, that does not mean they understand them all. Some, such as "Do not steal," are obvious. But others, such as "Do not covet," are just words on a page to them. We need to help students not only learn the Ten Commandments, but to understand them and recognize their impact on us today.

Use the bulletin board on page 4 throughout the study of the Ten Commandments as a visual reminder. Each lesson includes one of the Ten Commandments in the words of the Bible and also in simplified words to help children understand it. Discussion questions are provided to allow children to share their knowledge and ideas about the Ten Commandments. This discussion time will be a good opportunity for the teacher or parents to learn what the children know and what they need to be taught. The discussion is followed by a Bible story which illustrates the commandment and a related Bible verse which you may want to use for a memory verse. (*Note:* The New International Version is used for scripture references.) Each lesson also includes three or four pages of creative, fun activities to involve children in discovering important truths about each commandment. They will enjoy the puzzles, crafts, songs and rhymes, and other activities.

At the end of the ten lessons are two pages of ideas for culminating activities. Also, an answer key is provided at the back of the book.

As you teach these lessons, make sure that your children understand that obeying the Ten Commandments does not save anyone. In fact, no one except Jesus has ever been able to keep them all perfectly! The New Testament explains that the Ten Commandments were guidelines. They could not provide forgiveness. That is why God sent His Son Jesus to the earth, to set people free from sin. (See Romans 8:3–4.) Jesus enlarged upon the Ten Commandments. For example, he said that not only is murder wrong, but we are guilty of murder when we hate another person! He  summed up all Ten Commandments in two: "Love the Lord your God with all your heart and with all your soul and with all your mind," and "Love your neighbor as yourself." (Matthew 22:37, 39)

Be sure your children know that the Ten Commandments will not get them into heaven. The only way we can go to heaven is by placing our faith in Jesus. After we do that, we trust in Him, and we obey His commands because we love Him.

Ten Commandments
Bulletin Board

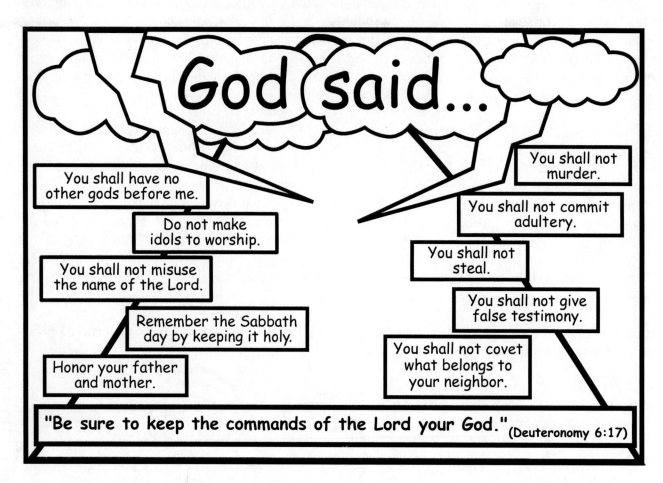

Directions

1. Cover the board with light blue paper.

2. Draw a large mountain on the paper or cut one from grey paper and mount it at the center of the board. Draw or cut out a dark cloud and lightning for the top of the mountain.

3. Print "GOD SAID . . ." in black across the top of the board.

4. Print the Bible verse at the bottom of the board or print it on a strip of paper and attach it to the board.

5. Cut 20 strips from different colors of construction paper.

6. Use a black marker to print the Ten Commandments on 10 of the paper strips.

7. Mount the Ten Commandments on the board in order as shown.

8. Print the numbers 1 through 10 on the remaining paper strips. Cover each commandment with the correct numbered strip of paper.

9. Uncover each commandment as students study it.

The First Commandment

God said, "You shall have no other gods before me." (Exodus 20:3)
In other words: Put God first in your life!

Discussion

God began His ten commandments by reminding His people of what He had done for them. What had He done? *(Have students read Exodus 20:1–2 to find out that God had brought His people out of slavery in Egypt.)* Why was it important for the people to remember this? *(They needed to realize that they owed God their obedience.)* When God's people got to the land He had promised them, they would encounter many ungodly people who worshipped idols of all kinds. God did not want them to be influenced to worship idols and follow the wrong pathways. He wanted and deserved their worship for Himself. Why does God deserve our worship and obedience?

Bible Story (1 Kings 3:9–11)

When King David died, his son Solomon became king of Israel. One night God appeared to Solomon in a dream and said, "Ask for whatever you want me to give you." Solomon made a very wise choice. He did not ask for great wealth or fame or power. He asked God for "a discerning heart," or wisdom. God was so pleased with his request, He not only made Solomon the wisest king the world had ever known, but also the wealthiest, and because of his great wisdom, he become famous and powerful. Solomon had it all—everything a person could ever want. But that did not keep him for disobeying God.

Solomon married more than 700 women! God was very displeased, but Solomon did not seem to care. Most of his wives were idol-worshipers and he not only let them worship their false gods; he even joined them! With all the blessings of God all around him, Solomon tried to worship both God and idols. Solomon knew the first commandment. He had heard it all of his life, but he ignored it and did what he wanted. Because of Solomon's disobedience of the first commandment, God split his kingdom in half. When Solomon died and his son became king, he ruled over a much smaller kingdom, called Judah, while another king ruled the larger kingdom of Israel.

King David gave his son some very good advice before he died. He said, "Observe what the Lord your God requires: Walk in his ways, and keep his decrees and commands, his laws and requirements, as written in the Law of Moses, so that you may prosper in all you do and wherever you go." (1 Kings 2:3) Solomon did not follow his father's advice. He did not give God first place in his life, and it cost him the kingdom.

Bible Verse

"Love the Lord your God with all your heart and with all your soul and with all your mind. This is the first and greatest command." (Matthew 22:37–38)

When people asked Jesus which was the greatest commandment, He did not hesitate to say that it was to love God completely. He knew that if we love God as much as we can, we will be eager to obey all His commands. Also, our love for Him will spill over into loving other people and treating them the way God wants us to. Do any of us really love God as much as we should? As much as we could? How can we learn to love Him more and give Him first place in our lives?

Our Great God

Directions: Why does God deserve to have first place in our lives? He is not like other gods or idols. To find out how He is different, read the sentences. Look up the Bible references (New International Version) to help you. Complete the acrostic with words that describe Him.

1. ___ **O** ___ ___ ___ ___ ___ ___
2. ___ **U** ___ ___ ___ ___ ___ ___ ___ ___ ___ ___
3. ___ **R** ___ ___ ___ ___ ___
4. ___ **G** ___ ___ ___
5. ___ **R** ___ ___ ___ ___ ___
6. ___ **E** ___ ___ ___ ___ ___
7. ___ **A** ___ ___ ___ ___ ___
8. ___ **T** ___ ___ ___
9. ___ ___ ___ ___ **G** ___ ___ ___ ___
10. ___ **O** ___ ___ ___ ___
11. ___ ___ ___ ___ **D**

1. O great and _____ God, whose name is the Lord Almighty, great are your purposes and mighty are your deeds. (Jeremiah 32:18b–19a)

2. Great is our Lord and mighty in power; his _____ has no limit. (Psalm 147:5)

3. The LORD is the everlasting God, the _____ of the ends of the earth. (Isaiah 40:28)

4. You are forgiving and _____, O Lord, abounding in love to all you who call to you. (Psalm 86:5)

5. Job said, "I know that my _____ lives." (Job 19:25a)

6. Abraham . . . called upon the name of the LORD, the _____ God. (Genesis 21:33)

7. O Lord, the great and _____ God, . . . we have sinned and done wrong. (Daniel 9:4–5a)

8. He is the _____ God and eternal life. (1 John 5:20b)

9. The LORD is slow to anger, abounding in love and _____ sin and rebellion. (Numbers 14:18a)

10. The LORD is faithful to all his promises and _____ toward all he has made. (Psalm 145:13b)

11. Everyone who calls on the name of the _____ will be saved. (Acts 2:21)

Put God First Action Rhyme

"Remember who I am," God said,

"And what I've done for you."

(Point to heaven, then to others.)

Then He told His people

What He wanted them to do.

(Wag index finger as if giving orders.)

"Put Me first and worship me.

Make Me number one.

(Hold up one index finger above your head.)

Give Me first place in your heart;

Of other gods, have none."

(Put hands over heart; then sweep hands down, palms down.)

That's the first commandment

God gave them to obey.

(Hold up one index finger.)

And we should still obey it now

Every hour of each day.

(Point to each other; then to imaginary watch on your wrist.)

Put God first! Worship Him!

Make Him number one.

(Hold up one index finger above your head.)

Give Him first place in your heart;

Of other gods, have none.

(Put hands over heart; then sweep hands down, palms down.)

God First Decoration

Materials

- crayons or colored markers
- scissors
- string or thread
- patterns below (two copies of the circle)
- cardboard
- glue
- sharp pointed pencil

Directions

1. Color both circles and both numbers (use light colors so the words show through); then cut them out.

2. Trace the circle and the number on cardboard and cut them out.

3. Glue the circles and numbers to the front and back of the cardboard pieces.

4. Use the sharp point of a pencil to poke a tiny hole in the top of the circle and the top of the number.

5. Use string or thread to attach the number at the center of the circle, leaving some extra at the top of the circle for a hanger.

6. Hang the decoration in your room or in a window.

The Second Commandment

God said, "Do not make idols nor bow down and worship them."   Exodus 20:4–5
In other words: Worship only God!

Discussion

God's first commandment was to have no other gods before Him. Of course, that meant no one was to worship idols. The first and second commandments are closely connected. What is the difference between God and idols or false gods? *(Idols and false gods are not alive; God is. Only God deserves our worship. Only He can hear us when we call on Him and help us. Idols are just statues that people have made. They cannot hear or see or move. God created us and knows everything about us. He has greater power than anybody or anything. He can do anything.)* Does anybody today worship idols? *(Let students share their ideas. They may mention idols such as money.)*

Bible Story (Exodus 32)

While Moses was up on Mount Sinai receiving the Ten Commandments from God, the people below were already breaking the second commandment! They said to Aaron, Moses' brother, "Make us gods who will go before us. As for this fellow Moses who brought us up out of Egypt, we do not know what has happened to him." Did Aaron scold them for wanting such a thing? Did he remind them they already had God to watch over them? No, Aaron did what they asked. He told the people to bring him whatever gold jewelry they had. When they had escaped Egypt, the Egyptians had given the Israelites jewelry and gold and silver cups and ornaments. Aaron took their gold and put it over a fire to melt it down. He probably carved a wooden shape like a calf first, then covered the wooden shape with gold. The people were thrilled with their idol. In Egypt, where they had lived for many years, idols of bulls and calves were everywhere. The Egyptians worshiped many different gods. Now God's people thought they could do the same thing. They worshiped the calf idol and sacrificed burnt offerings to it.

The Lord knew what His people were doing and sent Moses back down the mountain. Moses was so angry when he saw what the people were doing, he threw down the stone tablets on which the Ten Commandments were written and they broke. He grabbed the calf idol and burned it in the fire. Then he ground what was left of it to a powder, scattered it on water, and made the people drink it. When Moses asked Aaron why he had allowed the people to sin in such a way, Aaron blamed the people. Trying to make himself look innocent, Aaron said that when they brought him gold jewelry, he threw it into the fire and out came the golden calf! The Lord punished the people by making them very sick.

Bible Verse

"But the LORD is the true God; he is the living God, the eternal King." (Jeremiah 10:10a)

God proved over and over that He is the one true God who hears the prayers of His people, who comforts and helps and guides, and who sent His only Son to the earth to die for our sins. Idols can do nothing and do not deserve to be worshiped. Only God deserves to be worshiped.

Useless Idols

Directions: The Prophet Isaiah wrote about how silly it is for people to make idols, then worship what they have made. He said, "All who make idols are nothing, and the things they treasure are worthless." (Isaiah 44:9a) Read what Isaiah said below. Then find and circle the underlined words in the puzzle. Write the leftover letters from the puzzle in order on the lines for some good advice.

"The blacksmith takes a <u>tool</u> and works with it in the coals; he <u>shapes</u> an <u>idol</u> with <u>hammers</u>, he forges it with the might of his <u>arm</u> . . . . The carpenter measures with a line and makes an <u>outline</u> with a marker; he roughs it out with <u>chisels</u> and <u>marks</u> it with compasses. He shapes it in the <u>form</u> of <u>man</u>, of man in all his glory, that it may dwell in a <u>shrine</u>. He cut down cedars, or perhaps took a cypress or oak . . . . It is man's <u>fuel</u> for burning; some of it he takes and warms himself, he kindles a <u>fire</u> and bakes bread. But he also <u>fashions</u> a <u>god</u> and <u>worships</u> it; he makes an idol and <u>bows</u> down to it. Half of the wood he burns in the fire; . . . . From the rest he <u>makes</u> a god, his idol; he bows down to it and worships. He <u>prays</u> to it and says, 'Save me; you are my god.'" (Isaiah 44:12–17)

C	H	I	S	E	L	S	S	M	S	O
W	T	D	A	N	M	H	A	Y	S	U
O	K	O	E	S	A	I	A	K	H	T
R	D	L	O	P	O	R	R	F	R	L
S	F	U	E	L	P	A	L	A	I	I
H	I	S	B	F	M	S	G	S	N	N
I	R	O	D	O	D	M	A	H	E	E
P	E	O	D	R	W	E	M	I	A	M
S	G	N	W	M	O	S	R	O	A	S
M	A	K	E	S	H	I	P	N	R	G
O	H	A	M	M	E	R	S	S	M	D

— — — — — — — — — .

— — — — — — — — — — — .

— — — — — — — — — — — — !

How Many Gods?

Directions: To find out what Paul wrote about idols, follow the directions.

In the boxes below, cross out every word that <u>begins with **D**</u>, <u>rhymes with "here"</u>; and <u>ends with **P**</u>. Write the remaining words in order on the lines. Look up 1 Corinthians 8:4b to check your answer.

FEAR	WE	DO	KNOW	KEEP	CLEAR	THAT
AN	WRAP	IDOL	IS	STEER	DOES	NOTHING
AT	SHIP	DEAR	ALL	IN	TOP	THE
WORLD	APPEAR	DON'T	AND	THAT	THERE	NEAR
IS	NO	LEAP	GOD	BUT	DARE	ONE

— — — — — — — — — — — —

— — — — — — — — — —

— — — — — — — — —

— — — — — — — —

___ ___ ___   ___ ___ ___. (1 Corinthians 8:4b)

Love God Mobile

John, one of Jesus' disciples, wrote that we love God because He first loved us. Idols never loved anyone. They are not able to love, or do anything else. God knew that loving idols is a waste of time because they cannot love us back or help us in any way. When we love God, He loves us back. God even loves people who never love Him back.

Make this mobile to hang in your room as a reminder of God's love for you and your love for Him.

Materials

- patterns from page 13
- crayons or colored markers
- scissors
- hole punch
- two sheets of white paper

- wire clothes hanger (white if possible)
- string or thread
- glue
- stapler and staples
- cotton balls

Directions

1. Color the hearts with light colors so the words can still be read.

2. Cut out all eight hearts.

3. Glue or staple the same-sized hearts together, back to back along the edges. Leave the top of the hearts open.

4. Punch a hole in the top of each heart.

5. Take cotton balls and pull them out a bit to flatten them. Stuff the cotton in the tops of the hearts to make them puffy. Then glue or staple the tops of the hearts closed.

6. Cut two long cloud shapes exactly the same from the white paper.

7. Glue or staple the paper clouds on both sides of the wire clothes hanger, leaving the bottom open. The hook of the hanger should stick out above the clouds.

8. Tie different lengths of string or thread to the hearts; then tie the string or thread to the bottom of the clothes hanger.

9. Glue cotton balls on the white clouds.

Love God Mobile

I

LOVE

GOD

I love you,
O LORD,
my strength.

Psalm 18:1

ME

LOVES

GOD

How great is the love
that the Father
has lavished on us !
(1 John 3:1)

The Third Commandment

God said, "You shall not misuse the name of the Lord your God." (Exodus 20:7)
In other words: Speak God's name with reverence and respect!

Discussion

What are some ways you have heard people use God's name disrespectfully? *(Let students share without being explicit.)* Is it alright to tell jokes about God? Why is it important for us to speak God's name with reverence and respect? *(God is our Creator, our Father who loves us. He is more powerful and greater than anyone or anything. He deserves to be honored, not made fun of or insulted.)* People often say God's name without even thinking; it is just a habit. What should we do when we hear others misusing His name? How can we make sure we always give Him the respect He deserves? *(Read the Bible to get to know God better; talk to Him; ask Him to help us do what He wants.)*

Bible Story (2 Kings 18:17–19:37)

King Hezekiah was scared! The king of Assyria had sent his army to Jerusalem to attack and destroy it. Hezekiah sent word of his problem to God's prophet Isaiah to ask him to pray and ask God for help. Isaiah sent this message to the king: "Do not be afraid . . . Listen! I am going to put such a spirit in him that when he hears a certain report, he will return to his own country." Shortly after that, the Assyrian commander led his army away from Jerusalem. The king sent a letter to Hezekiah: "Do not let the god you depend upon deceive you when he says 'Jerusalem will not be handed over to the king of Assyria.' Surely you have heard what the kings of Assyria have done to all the countries, destroying them completely." He wanted to make sure that Hezekiah did not think his troubles were over just because the Assyrian army had pulled back from Jerusalem. When King Hezekiah read the letter, he took it to the temple of the Lord and spread it out before the Lord. Then he prayed, asking God to protect Jerusalem from the wicked Assyrians.

God gave Isaiah a message of encouragement for Hezekiah. God said that the king of Assyria had spoken against God and insulted Him. The ungodly king spoke God's name disrespectfully, and God was going to punish him. God promised Hezekiah that the king of Assyria would not enter Jerusalem or even fight against it. God would defend the city. That very night, He punished the wicked, disrespectful Assyrians. He sent an angel to their camp and put to death 185 thousand of them! When the soldiers woke up the next morning, dead bodies were everywhere with no clue about how they had died. The king of Assyria took what was left of his army and went home and stayed there. Later when he was worshiping an idol in his temple, his two sons sneaked in and killed him. The king who misused God's holy name paid for his sin.

Bible Verse

"Glorify the LORD with me; let us exalt his name together." (Psalm 34:3)

God's name is holy and instead of using it carelessly or saying it disrespectfully, we should praise and honor (exalt) His name. Another verse in the Bible says that His name is "majestic" and we should "magnify" it. What do you think that means? *(Lift it up with reverence, say good things about God, and worship Him.)*

God's Holy Name Song

(*Tune:* "I Will Make You Fishers of Men")

If you want to honor the Lord,

Honor the Lord, honor the Lord,

If you want to honor the Lord,

Praise His holy name.

Praise His holy name, praise His holy name.

If you want to honor the Lord,

Praise His holy name.

Always say God's name carefully,

Respectfully, and reverently.

Always say God's name carefully

Praise His holy name.

Praise His holy name, praise His holy name.

Always say God's name carefully.

Praise His holy name.

Worship God because He's the King

Of everyone and everything.

He deserves the honor we bring;

Praise His holy name.

Praise His holy name, praise His holy name.

Worship God because He's the King.

Praise His holy name.

Names of God

Directions: God has many different names. Each one is special and tells us something important about Him. Use the code to discover some names for God.

CODE

A	B	C	D	E	F	G	H	I	J	K	L	M
▶	✳	†	◆	✠	✱	♠	♥	➤	↔	✾	)	■

N	O	P	Q	R	S	T	U	V	W	X	Y	Z
✓	✗	✚	✏	□	★	▼	✌	✳	⇨	❀	'	'

) ✗ □ ◆   (Exodus 6:2a)

† □ ✠ ▶ ▼ ✗ □   (Deuteronomy 32:6b)

✱ ▶ ▼ ♥ ✠ □   (Deuteronomy 32:6b)

■ ✗ ★ ▼   ♥ ➤ ♠ ♥   (Psalm 46:4)

★ ▶ ✱ ➤ ✗ □   (Psalm 65:5)

□ ✗ † ✾   (Psalm 78:35)

□ ✠ ◆ ✠ ✠ ■ ✠ □   (Psalm 78:35)

★ ♥ ✠ ✚ ♥ ✠ □ ◆   (Psalm 80:1)

The Fourth Commandment

God said, "Remember the Sabbath day by keeping it holy." (Exodus 20:8)
In other words: Keep the Lord's Day holy!

Discussion

When God created the world, He worked for six days and rested on the seventh. When He gave the Ten Commandments to Moses, God included a command for His people to do the same, to set aside a day to rest from their work and to meet together to worship Him. Hundreds of years later, Jesus died on Friday, then rose from the dead on Sunday. After that, Christians began setting aside Sunday, Jesus' resurrection day, as the day to rest from work and worship God. Most Jewish people still celebrate Saturday as the Sabbath. Ask students if they think we keep our Sabbath day holy today? Does everyone rest from work on the Sabbath? Why or why not? Have them give some examples. How much time do we spend worshiping God together on our Sabbath? What other activities do we do on that day? Take a vote to see if students think God is pleased or displeased with the way Christians keep the Sabbath today. Then let students share the reasons for their votes.

Bible Story (Exodus 16)

After Moses led his people out of Egypt, they wandered around in the desert for 40 years before they found the Promised Land. During that time, God took care of them and provided their needs. When the people complained to Moses that they had eaten better food back in Egypt, God told Moses He would rain down bread from heaven for them. The people woke up one morning to find small white flakes on the ground everywhere. They had never seen anything like it. Moses said, "It is the bread the Lord has given you to eat." They picked it up and tasted it. It tasted like wafers made with honey. The people called it "manna," which means "What is it?" Moses told the people that God's instructions were for each family to gather enough manna to feed every person in the family for one day. No one was to gather extra for the next day. Only enough manna for one day–that was God's rule. Of course, some lazy people disobeyed and gathered extra so they wouldn't have to go out and pick it up every day. But the next morning their bread from heaven did not smell very heavenly! It was full of bugs and had to be thrown out. God made sure they obeyed His instructions.

On the day before the Sabbath, the people were to gather enough manna to feed their families for two days so they would have enough for the Sabbath day too. God warned them that there would be no manna on the ground on the Sabbath day. Some disobedient people went out on the Sabbath day to pick up manna, but there was not any. God had told His people to rest from their work on the Sabbath, and that included gathering manna. If they were too lazy to gather enough for two days on the day before the Sabbath, they would just have to go hungry until the day after the Sabbath when the manna would appear again. For 40 years God provided manna every day except on the Sabbath to feed His people.

Bible Verse

"This is the day the Lord has made; let us rejoice and be glad in it." (Psalm 118:24)

We should thank God for every day, but especially for a day when we can rest and worship Him.

Remember This!

Directions: What did God want His people to remember on the Sabbath day of rest? To find out, use words from the word box to complete the Bible verses. Some words will be used more than once.

WORD BOX

brought	work	rested	creating	Egypt
arm	slaves	Lord	holy	blessed

By the seventh day God had finished the _____ he had been doing;

so on the seventh day he _____ from all his _____.

And God _____ the seventh day and made it _____,

because on it he _____ from all the _____ of

_____ that he had done. (Genesis 2:2–3)

Remember that you were _____ in _____

and that the _____ your God _____ you out

of there with a mighty hand and an outstretched _____. Therefore, the

_____ your God has commanded you to observe the Sabbath day.

(Deuteronomy 5:15)

What do you think about on your Sabbath day? Do you think about the great things God has done? Do you thank Him for saving you from slavery to sin?_____

_____

Just for You and Me

Did God rest after creating the world because he was tired? Of course not. The Bible tells us that God is all-powerful and never gets tired. But people do. You and I need to rest both our bodies and our minds sometimes. Some Jewish religious leaders made up all kinds of extra rules about the Sabbath and scolded people when they did not obey them. They gave Jesus a hard time because He did not always do what they thought he should do on the Sabbath.

Directions: Read the story about Jesus and the Pharisees in Mark 2:23–26. Then complete the picture below by writing in the speech balloon what Jesus said about the Sabbath.

The Sabbath was made for _____, not _____ for the Sabbath. So the Son of Man is _____ even of the Sabbath. (Mark 2:27–28)

What do you think Jesus meant? _____

_____

Sabbath Day Finger Play

1–2–3–4–5–6–7 days in every week,

(*Hold up a finger for each number.*)

Lots of time to work and play, to laugh and sing and speak.

(*Smack two fists together, hold up a hand and jiggle fingers, hold stomach and laugh, hold out both arms, then point to mouth.*)

God wants us to put aside one day each week for rest,

(*Lean head on both hands and close your eyes.*)

To spend some time praising Him and giving Him our best.

(*Hold both hands toward heaven, then point up with one finger.*)

A day to meet with others to worship God above,

(*Fold hands and look up toward heaven.*)

To read His Word and talk to Him and thank Him for His love.

(*Hold both hands like an open Bible, then bow your head, close your eyes, and fold your hands.*)

One day a week, one seventh of our time; that isn't much.

(*Hold up seven fingers and touch one.*)

To put aside to catch our breath and feel His loving touch.

(*Take a deep breath, then put your hand on your heart.*)

The Fifth Commandment

God said, "Honor your father and mother." (Exodus 20:12)
In other words: Respect and obey your parents!

Discussion

Ask students what it means to honor our parents. Their answers should include obedience and respect. Point out that God puts human mothers and fathers in charge of babies to take care of their needs and help them grow into adults. God has a perfect plan for each of us and that includes putting us in families that are just right for us. God calls Himself our heavenly Father and He says He comforts us as a mother comforts her child. Parents and children are important to God. Ask students to brainstorm things their parents do for them (providing their needs, loving them, protecting them from harm, taking care of them when they are sick or hurt, etc.). Our parents deserve our respect and honor. It pleases God when we obey them.

Bible Story (Luke 2:41–52)

When Jesus was 12 years old Mary and Joseph took Him with them on their yearly trip to the temple in Jerusalem. At age 12 He was old enough to study the Old Testament and understand the importance of obeying God. Jesus and his parents probably traveled to the big city and back home with a large group of friends and neighbors, so when Mary and Joseph did not see him on the trip back they did not think anything of it. But when the day ended and Jesus still could not be found, His parents got frightened. What if something had happened to Him? What if He was lost in the big city? The couple hurried back to Jerusalem and began looking everywhere for their son. Three days later they found Jesus in the temple listening to the religious teachers who were amazed at how well He understood the Scriptures. By that time Joseph and Mary were at their wits' end! "Son, why have you treated us like this?" Mary asked Him.

Jesus was suprised at His parents' concern. Time had passed quickly for Him in the temple. He probably had not even noticed that His parents weren't around. "Didn't you know I had to be in my Father's house?" He asked them. They did not understand, but were ready to take Jesus back home. He did not argue with them or beg to stay just a little longer. Rather Jesus "went down to Nazareth with them and was obedient to them." (Luke 2:51) Jesus was the Son of God, the Creator of the Universe, but He obediently did what His earthly parents told Him. He honored them and respected Mary and Joseph as the parents God had chosen for Him.

Bible Verse

"Children, obey your parents in the Lord, for this is right." (Ephesians 6:1)

Honoring our parents means obeying them even when they are not around. To do something that you know your mom and dad would not permit you to do is disobedience both toward them and toward God.

Parent-Child Situations

Directions: Divide students into small groups. Cut out the real-life situations on this page and give one to each group. Have each group read its situation, then discuss together if it shows honor or dishonor to the parents. After 10 minutes or so, have each group share its ideas with the rest of the groups.

Situation 1

Janna's parents came to the school band concert especially to hear her play a flute solo. When her solo was finished, her dad clapped so loud it embarrassed Janna. After the concert a friend said to Janna, "Boy, your dad was really proud of you, wasn't he?"

Janna rolled her eyes and replied, "Sometimes my dad is really weird!" Then she found her parents and hurried them off before anyone could meet them.

Situation 2

Carlos knew his mom did not like the guys with whom he hung around. When he said they wanted him to go to a party with them on Saturday night, his mom said he could not go. "You promised to help Mrs. Anderson move her furniture," she said. "Besides, I do not like you being around those tough kids." On Saturday evening while Carlos' mom was working, he went over to Mrs. Anderson's apartment and quickly moved her furniture. Then he hurried off to spend the evening with his friends at the party.

Situation 3

Sophie begged and begged to have her friend Marcy over to spend the night, but her mom kept saying that she was just too tired after her long day of work to have her over that night. "Let's wait until the weekend," her mom said. Sophie blew her top and told her mom she was selfish and never let her have any fun! Then she stomped out of the house, slamming the door.

Situation 4

Jason's cousin took him and a couple of friends to a popular movie. When they got there, Jason realized it was a movie that his father had talked to him about just the week before. He had said it was not a movie that a Christian should see. Jason tried to talk the other boys into going somewhere else, but they refused. Instead, they tried to convince him that it was okay to go to the movie. "We won't tell your mom or dad. Nobody will ever know," his cousin promised. Jason was tempted, but decided to have the others pick him up at the library across the street when they were finished.

Obedience Blossom

Materials

- patterns on this page
- colored markers or crayons
- scissors
- hole punch
- brad fastener

Directions

1. Copy this page and have students color lightly and cut out the seven flower petals.

2. Have them stack the petals together with the narrow part on the bottom.

3. Use a hole punch to punch a hole near the bottom of the petals. (You may need to punch three or four petals at a time.)

4. Show students how to insert the brad in the holes and bend it at the back to secure the petals together.

5. Have them spread the petals of the blossom apart to read the Bible verse.

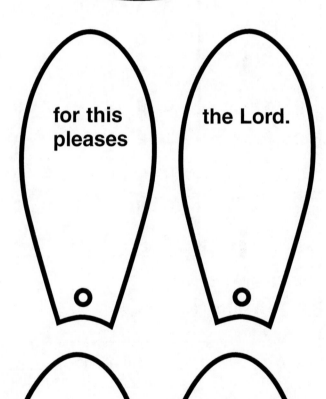

Colossians 3:20

for this pleases

the Lord.

Children

obey

your parents

in everything,

What God Says About Parents

Directions: Look up the Bible verses (New International Version) and fill in the missing words. Then find and circle those words in the word search puzzle. Write the leftover letters in order on the lines to find out what God wants you to do.

```
D  T  E  A  C  H  I  N  G  N  I
G  I  O  D  W  A  N  T  O  S  N
W  I  S  E  Y  O  E  I  U  T  S
O  A  L  C  *  S  S  W  A  Y  T
F  O  O  L  I  S  H  S  O  B  R
E  Y  Y  P  A  P  R  I  D  E  U
O  U  S  P  F  R  L  I  F  E  C
J  E  M  E  P  A  R  I  E  N  T
D  O  I  T  S  A  S  J  N  E  I
C  R  Y  S  U  S  D  I  D  E  O
G  C  O  M  P  A  S  S  I  O  N
```

1. Parents are the _____ of their children. (Proverbs 17:6b)

2. As a father has _____ on his children, so the Lord has

   _____ on those who fear him. (Psalm 103:13)

3. A _____ son brings _____ to his father, but a _____

   son _____ to his mother. (Proverbs 10:1)

4. Listen to your father, who gave you _____, and do not _____

   your mother when she is old. (Proverbs 23:22)

5. A fool spurns his father's _____. (Proverbs 15:5a)

6. Listen, my son, to your father's _____ and do not forsake

   your mother's _____. (Proverbs 1:8)

   What God wants you to do: ___ ___ ___ ___ ___ ___ ___ ___

   ___ ___ ___ ___ ___ ___ ___ ___ ___ ___ ___

   ___ ___ ___ ___ ___ ___ ___ ___ ___ ___ ___ ___

   ___ ___ ___ ___ ___ ___ ___ ___ ___ ___ .

The Sixth Commandment

God said, "You shall not murder." (Exodus 20:13)
In other words: Do not murder anyone!

Discussion

God created life and He says He is the only one who should decide when to end life. In the New Testament the apostle John said we break this commandment if we hate someone. Why is hating another person so wrong? Does God hate anyone? No, God loves everyone, even the worst sinner. If a person murders another person, can he or she ever be forgiven? Discuss how God offers His forgiveness to everyone. Our sins were paid for by Jesus' death on the cross.

Bible Story (Genesis 4:1–16)

Cain and Abel were the very first brothers in the world, sons of Adam and Eve. Abel was a shepherd who raised sheep and Cain was a farmer who liked to grow fruits and vegetables. Adam and Eve taught their sons how to offer sacrifices to God. When Abel offered sacrifices from his flock of sheep, God was pleased with his offering. The book of Hebrews in the New Testament says that Abel was a righteous man. God looked on Abel with favor. But when Cain made an offering to God, perhaps of some of the things he had grown, God was not pleased. The way Cain responded shows us that Cain's heart was not right with God. In fact, God said to Cain, "If you do what is right, will you not be accepted?" Cain became angry when God did not favor him as He favored Abel. His heart was not right, so neither was his sacrifice.

Cain invited his brother to go out in the field with him; then he attacked Abel and killed him. Why? Was Cain jealous of his brother because God favored him? Or was Cain just mad at God and taking out his anger on his brother? We do not know why; we only know that Cain did a terrible thing. Did he think he could hide his sin from God? The Lord knew exactly what Cain had done. "Where is your brother?" God asked him.

"I do not know," Cain told God. "Am I my brother's keeper?" Cain did not seem to be sorry for the murder he had committed. Then God told him that his sin was already known. He punished Cain by taking away his work, the way he made his living. "When you work the ground, it will no longer yield its crops for you." God told him, "You will be a restless wanderer on the earth." Cain was afraid that people would find out what he had done and they would kill him. So God graciously put a special mark on Cain so that no one would kill him. The Bible does not tell us what that mark was, but it was God's way of protecting Cain even though he had committed such a horrible act.

Bible Verse

"Anyone who hates his brother is a murderer." (1 John 3:15)

Hatred is a terrible attitude that sometimes leads to murder, but even if the act of murder is not actually committed, God considers the person who hates the same as a murderer!

Life Is Precious

Directions: Why is a person's life so precious? To find out, read the Bible verses below. Then follow the directions.

> "Then God said, 'Let us make man in our image, in our likeness, and let them rule over the fish of the sea and the birds of the air, over the livestock, over all the earth, and over all the creatures that move along the ground.' So God created man in his own image, in the image of God he created him; male and female he created them." (Genesis 1:26–27)
>
> "The Lord God formed the man from the dust of the ground and breathed into his nostrils the breath of life, and the man became a living being." (Genesis 2:7)
>
> "The Spirit of God has made me; the breath of the Almighty gives me life." (Job 33:4)

1. Underline the words that tell us in whose image we were created.

2. Circle what God gave people.

3. Underline, with two lines, the words that indicate from what we were created.

4. Write on the lines in your own words why killing a person is different from killing an animal.

_____

_____

_____

_____

He Made Us

Directions: Complete the poem with the correct rhyming words.

God made people; yes, it's true.

He created me and _____.

He planned each person carefully,

Knew what He wanted us to _____.

The animals He made are fine,

But our spirits, yours and _____,

Aren't like theirs, not in the least.

I'm a person, not a _____!

God gave the breath of life to man;

That was His eternal _____,

In God's image, for His glory,

Made to love Him; that's our _____!

Directions: Write your own prayer to thank God for making you in His image and for loving you the way you are.

_____

_____

_____

_____

Heart Thoughts Craft

Materials

- a copy of this page for each student
- colored markers or crayons
- scissors
- glue

Directions

1. Color the heart pattern and cut it out.

2. Fold the pattern on the broken lines. Glue the tab on the inside to make a heart pocket.

3. Cut out the title word strip and glue it to the front of the heart pocket.

4. Cut out the other word strips and fold them in half.

5. Put the folded strips in the heart pocket. Take one out each day to read and think about.

**LIFE IS FRAGILE.
HANDLE IT WITH CARE!**

- - - - - - - - - - - - - - - - - - - -

(title word strip)

- - - - - - - - - - - - - - - - - - - -

God made people for His pleasure! Are you pleasing Him?

- - - - - - - - - - - - - - - - - - - -

Murder begins in a person's heart. (I John 3:15)

- - - - - - - - - - - - - - - - - - - -

God says don't hate anyone. Instead, love people as He does.

- - - - - - - - - - - - - - - - - - - -

God created us like Him! How are you like God?

- - - - - - - - - - - - - - - - - - - -

God loves people so much He sent Jesus to die for us all.

- - - - - - - - - - - - - - - - - - - -

Respect life because it is from God.

- - - - - - - - - - - - - - - - - - - -

Jesus said to love your neighbor as much as you love yourself.

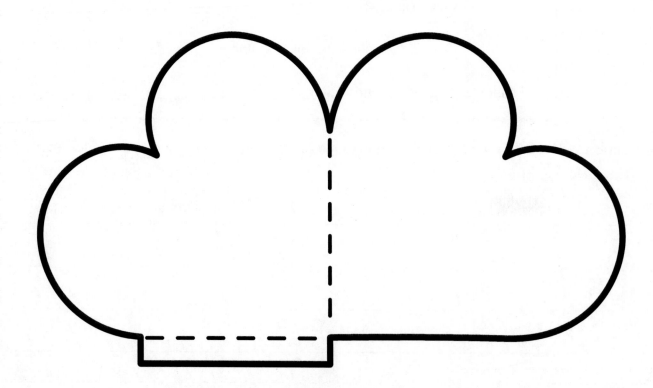

The Seventh Commandment

God said, "You shall not commit adultery." (Exodus 20:14)
In other words: Be faithful to your husband or wife.

Discussion

God created marriage to be a special relationship between a man and a woman for the rest of their lives. His seventh commandment means that husbands and wives should be faithful to each other. What do you think that means? *(Let students share their ideas without being explicit in their details.)* A husband and wife should love each other and be loyal. What happens to a family when a husband or wife decides he or she loves someone new? *(Let students share ideas such as the following: the husband and wife divorce; the family splits apart; the children do not get to see one of the parents as much; the whole family is sad or angry.)* Adultery is a selfish sin and God knew how much it would hurt people. He does not want people to hurt each other.

Bible Story (2 Samuel 11–12)

King David had everything a man could want, but one evening he saw something he did not have and he wanted it. What he wanted was a beautiful woman named Bathsheba. She was married, and so was David, but he did not let that stop him. King David sent for her to come to his palace, and they committed adultery. Later, Bathsheba sent a message to David to tell him she was going to have his baby. David had to figure out a solution to that problem fast! He sent for Uriah, Bathsheba's husband, who was away fighting in Israel's army. When Uriah came, David talked with him, then sent him home to his wife. But Uriah would not go inside his home to spend the night with his wife because he said he felt guilty enjoying himself while his fellow soldiers were risking their lives in great discomfort. Nothing David could say would convince Uriah to spend time with his wife. Soon Uriah would find out that his wife was pregnant and that it was not his child. Then what would he do? Finally, David sent Uriah back to the fighting with a note for his general. The note told General Joab to put Uriah in the front lines of the fighting so he would be killed. Joab obeyed and before long Bathsheba received word that her husband had been killed in battle. She was sad, but King David brought her to live with him as his wife in the palace. David had not only committed adultery, he had also murdered Uriah by arranging for his death. He had broken two of God's ten commandments.

God sent His prophet Nathan to talk with David. Finally, David admitted his sin and asked God for forgiveness. God forgave him and Bathsheba, but he punished them for their sin by letting their baby get sick and die. David's family was also hurt by David's sin. His children rebelled against God and turned against their father and one another. And David had started the whole mess!

Bible Verse

"Each one of you also must love his wife as he loves himself, and the wife must respect her husband." (Ephesians 5:33)

Husbands and wives should be faithful to God and also faithful to each other.

God's Plan for Marriage

Directions: What does God want in a marriage? Read the Bible verses; then match each one with the correct feature of marriage it describes.

_____ **1.** Do not be yoked together with unbelievers. For what do righteousness and wickedness have in common? Or what fellowship can light have with darkness? . . . What does a believer have in common with an unbeliever? (2 Corinthians 6:14)

A. Time Spent Together

_____ **2.** May you rejoice in the wife of your youth. (Proverbs 5:18b)

B. Joy

_____ **3.** Each one of you also must love his wife as he loves himself, and the wife must respect her husband. (Ephesians 5:33)

C. Unity

_____ **4.** For this reason a man will leave his father and mother and be united to his wife, and the two will become one flesh. (Matthew 19:5)

D. Faithfulness and Determination to Stay Together

_____ **5.** If a man has recently married, he must not be sent to war or have any other duty laid on him. For one year he is to be free to stay at home and bring happiness to the wife he has married. (Deuteronomy 24:5)

E. Love and Respect

_____ **6.** They are no longer two, but one. Therefore, what God has joined together, let man not separate. (Matthew 19:6)

F. Common Faith in God

Marriage Maze

Directions: God wants people who get married to stay married until one or both die. There are many obstacles that can break up a marriage. Help the bride and groom find their way through the maze to a lifetime together.

Joseph's Story

Directions: Joseph's jealous brothers sold him into slavery in Egypt. In a strange, ungodly land, away from all his friends and families, Joseph was determined to obey God no matter what. But it was not easy. Look at the pictures and read Joseph's story. Number the pictures from 1 to 6 to show the order in which they happened. You can read the story in Genesis 39:1–21.

_____ Potiphar put Joseph in charge of everything he owned because he trusted him.

_____ Potiphar's wife liked the way Joseph looked. She tried to talk him into commiting adultery with her, but he refused.

_____ Joseph became a slave in the house of Potiphar, an Egyptian official. God gave Joseph success in everything he did.

_____ Potiphar's wife told him that Joseph had attacked her, but had run when she screamed for help. She showed him Joseph's cloak as proof.

_____ One day Potiphar's wife grabbed him when no one else was around. Joseph ran away, leaving his cloak in her hands.

_____ Potiphar believed his wife and had innocent Joseph thrown into prison.

Potiphar's wife was the sinful one. Joseph was punished though he had done nothing wrong. Read Genesis 39:21–23 to find out how God blessed Joseph.

The Eighth Commandment

God said, "You shall not steal." (Exodus 20:15)
In other words: Do not take anything that doesn't belong to you!

Discussion

Why do you think God hates stealing? Does it make a difference if you steal from someone who is rich instead of someone who is poor? Our service for God includes both what we do not do and what we do—do not do wrong, but do right. What is the opposite of stealing? *(Sharing and being generous with others.)* Ask students to share practical ideas for sharing and being generous.

Bible Story (1 Kings 21:1–22)

King Ahab was a wicked, idol-worshiping king. He had everything a person could want, but he wanted more. A man named Naboth owned a vineyard near Ahab's palace. Ahab had tried to buy it, but Naboth would not sell the property which was a family inheritance. King Ahab became angry when he could not get what he wanted, so he went to bed and pouted and refused to eat. When his wife, Jezebel, found out what his problem was, she promised to get the vineyard for him. She wrote letters in the king's name to city officials where Naboth lived. She told them to get two dishonest men to accuse Naboth in public of cursing God and the king. Then they should take Naboth out and stone him to death for what he had done (though the charges were made up). The officials did what Jezebel instructed and it was not long before word came back that Naboth was dead. Jezebel went and told her husband, "Naboth is dead and the vineyard is all yours." King Ahab hurried down to take possession of his new vineyard.

God told His prophet Elijah to meet Ahab in the vineyard and give him a message. When the two met, Elijah said to King Ahab, "You have sold yourself to do evil in the eyes of the Lord. God is going to bring disaster on you and your family for what you have done." Ahab suddenly realized how he had sinned and he was sorry for what he had done. Because he repented, God showed mercy to him. He waited until after Ahab was dead to bring disaster on his family. Ahab had broken two of God's commandments—he had stolen and he had murdered, even though it was not his hand that did either deed, he went along with the sin and benefited from it.

Bible Verse

"He who has been stealing must steal no longer, but must work, doing something useful with his own hands, that he may have something to share with those in need." (Ephesians 4:28)

This Bible verse includes both the do and the do not of God's eighth commandment—do not steal; do share. Instead of taking what belongs to someone else, we need to share what God has given us.

Generosity Rap

Everyone knows that you shouldn't steal,

And most of us don't, but here's the deal:

Not doing wrong is important, it's true,

But what really counts is the good that you do.

If you love the Lord and Jesus His Son,

Pleasing Him will be number one!

So, go ahead and obey all the Lord's do-nots,

But do the opposite too; yes, give it a shot.

Don't take from others, but start to give.

Share what you have, that's the way to live.

All that you have is from God above,

So sharing it all is sharing His love!

Be generous! Yah, that's the thing to do.

Share what God has given you—

Money, toys, food and clothes—

Don't hold so tightly onto those,

You can show that your love for Jesus is real

When you cheerfully share (the opposite of steal)!

A Thief Who Changed

Directions: Fill in the missing words in the puzzle to complete the story of Zacchaeus. **A** words go across; **D** words go down. Look up the Bible verses (New International Version) if you need help.

Zacchaeus lived in the city of **1-D**. (Luke 19:1)

His job was collecting **5-D** for the government. (Luke 19:2)

Zacchaeus **4-A** people by collecting more than needed and keeping the extra for himself. (Luke 19:8)

Because of his stealing, he was a **3-D** man. (Luke 19:2)

When Zacchaeus heard Jesus was coming to town, he climbed a **2-A** because he was too **6-D** to see over the crowd that was lined up along the road. (Luke 19:3–4)

Jesus saw Zacchaeus and told him to come down so He could go to his house. The crowd complained that Jesus was going to be the guest of a **9-A**. Everyone must have known about Zacchaeus' dishonesty. (Luke 19:7)

Zacchaeus believed in Jesus and it changed his life. He promised to give **7-A** of his possessions to the poor and to pay people back **8-D** times the amount of money he had stolen from them.

Zacchaeus did exactly what God says he wants us to do: he quit stealing and started sharing.

People Who Stole

Directions: Read in the Bible about some people who took what didn't belong to them and what happened to them. Use the code to figure out who these thieves were. Look up the Bible verses to check your answers.

A	B	C	D	E	F	G	H	I	J	K	L	M
🍎	❑	✔	☛	❃	✝	✳	☆	◆	✚	❀	↔	●

N	O	P	Q	R	S	T	U	V	W	X	Y	Z
❖	○	✈	✕	◼	➤	☎	▼	✐	✠	◆	■	↕

1. This man is one of Jesus' disciples. This man was a thief. He kept the money bag for the disciples and stole from it. Later he betrayed Jesus, then killed himself. (John 12:4–6)

2. After this man helped destroy Jericho, he disobeyed God's orders and stole some silver and gold he found in the city. His punishment was death. (Joshua 7:19–26)

3. When she and her husband Jacob left her father's home, she secretly took the household gods (idols) and hid them in her saddle. This caused an angry argument between her husband and father. (Genesis 31:19–42)

   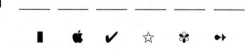

4. This man tricked his twin brother and stole his birthright and his blessing. His brother was so angry, he had to run for his life. Years later his brother forgave him. (Genesis 27:6–46)

The Ninth Commandment

God said, "You shall not give false testimony against your neighbor." (Exodus 20:16)
In other words: Do not tell lies about people.

Discussion

What is false testimony? *(Let students share their ideas.)* We usually hear false testimony related to a court trial. The "witnesses" give testimony (tell what they know) about the person being tried or about what happened. If a "witness" gives false testimony (is dishonest when questioned) he or she will be punished. What is gossip? *(Let students share their ideas.)* Sometimes people pass along information about another person. As other people pass along what they heard, nobody stops to consider that it might not be true. Great harm can be done by gossip or false testimony. People's reputations can be ruined.

Bible Story (Mark 14:53–65)

Some Jewish religious leaders hated Jesus and wanted to get rid of Him. They had Him arrested and put Him on trial, though they had already decided Jesus was guilty and they were going to have Him put to death. Many men told lies about Jesus, but their testimonies did not agree, so it was easy to see that they were not telling the truth. Then some other false witnesses stood up and said, "We heard Him say He would destroy the temple and build another one in three days!" Anyone who had been with Jesus knew that was false testimony. What Jesus had actually said was, "Destroy this temple, and I will raise it again in three days." (John 2:19) But He was not talking of the temple building; He was talking about His own body.

Jesus said nothing, so the high priest stood up and asked Him if He was going to answer the false accusations made against Him. Jesus still said nothing. But when the high priest asked Him if He was the Christ, the Son of the Blessed One, Jesus quietly answered, "I am." That made the high priest very angry because he did not believe Jesus was the Son of God. The high priest said they did not need any more witnesses to testify because everyone had heard what He had said and knew He was guilty of blasphemy, lying and being disrespectful of God. If Jesus had not truly been God's Son, He would have been guilty of blasphemy but since He was, His words were the truth. No one there believed the truth, so the trial ended with Jesus being condemned to death.

Bible Verse

"The Lord detests lying lips, but he delights in men who are truthful." (Proverbs 12:22)

God wants us to be honest in every area of our lives. Our lies can hurt others so easily.

False Witnesses

Directions: What does God have to say about false witnesses? To find out, write every word in the number 1 boxes in order on the number 1 lines (working in a left-to-right direction). Then write the number 2 words on the number 2 lines. Continue until all the words have been written on the correct numbered lines. Then look up Proverbs 14:5; 19:9 to check your work.

DOES	A	DECEIVE	TRUTHFUL	NOT	BUT	WITNESS
4	1	1	2	5	2	3
A	WITNESS	LIES	OUT	FALSE	POURS	WITNESS
3	5	3	2	4	1	1
WILL	A	GO	FALSE	AND	NOT	HE
2	4	4	5	1	3	2
POURS	UNPUNISHED	LIES	WILL	WHO	PERISH	OUT
4	5	1	2	3	3	5

_____ _____ _____ _____
  1   2   3   4

_____ _____, _____ _____
  5   1   2   3   4

_____ _____ _____ _____.
  5   1   2   3

(Proverbs 14:5)

_____ _____ _____ _____
  4   5   1   2

_____ _____ _____, _____ _____
  3   4   5   1   2

_____ _____ _____ _____
  3   4   5   1

(Proverbs 19:9)

_____ _____.
  2   3

Honesty Song

Directions: Sing this song together; then let students make up actions to go along with the words. Sing it together again with everyone doing the actions.

(*Tune:* "If You're Happy and You Know It")

If you want to please the Lord, tell the truth.

If you want to please the Lord, tell the truth.

God hates dishonesty; He wants truth from you and me,

So if you want to please the Lord, tell the truth.

Never tell lies about anyone.

Never tell lies about anyone.

God never wants you to hurt anyone, it's true.

Never tell lies about anyone.

If you can't say something nice, just keep still.

If you can't say something nice, just keep still.

Lies are wrong, don't you see, 'cause words can hurt so easily.

If you can't say something nice, just keep still.

Honesty Bookmark

Materials

- patterns on this page
- colored markers or crayons
- scissors
- glue

Directions

1. Cut out the two patterns for the bookmark and color them lightly.

2. Carefully cut the mouth open by cutting along the broken lines.

3. Glue the back of Pattern A to the front of Pattern B. Put glue around the edges only. Do not put glue on the back of the mouth.

4. When the glue has dried, read the bookmark. Carefully flip up the mouth to read the commandment underneath.

Finish Product

Pattern A

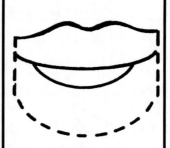

ALWAYS SPEAK THE TRUTH!

If you can't say something nice about a person, don't say anything at all!

Pattern B

You shall not give false testimony against your neighbor.
(Exodus 20:16)

The Tenth Commandment

God said, "You shall not covet anything that belongs to your neighbor." (Exodus 20:17)
In other words: Do not want what other people have!

Discussion

What does it mean to covet? *(Let students share their ideas; then explain that to covet is to want what someone else has.)* Coveting is an envious, greedy attitude. What is the opposite of coveting? *(Let students share their ideas. If they need help, suggest some words, such as contentment and generosity.)*

Bible Story (Genesis 25:21–34; 27:1–40)

Jacob and Esau were Isaac and Rebekah's twin sons. Esau was the older boy. He loved hunting and being outdoors. Jacob was quiet and liked to stay close to home. Because he was the oldest, according to Jewish tradition Esau would get the family birthright and his father's special blessing. The birthright gave the oldest son leadership over his brothers and he inherited twice as much when his father died. Esau did not care about his birthright, but Jacob coveted it. He wanted to have it and he got it. One day when Esau came home from hunting, he was very hungry. Jacob was cooking stew and Esau asked for some. That is when Jacob saw his chance. He told Esau he would give him some stew in exchange for his birthright. Esau did not stop to think about it; he was only concerned about getting something to eat. He agreed and Jacob gave him a bowl of stew. Jacob did not trick Esau, but Esau made a foolish bargain and Jacob got what he had wanted so much.

The birthright was legally Jacob's, but he also coveted the blessing his older brother would receive from their father. This time Jacob tricked both his father and his brother to get what he coveted. When Isaac was ready to give the blessing, Jacob disguised himself like Esau and took some cooked meat to his father. Isaac was almost blind, so he could not see that it was Jacob, not Esau. After Isaac ate, he blessed Jacob with the blessing for the oldest son of the family. Not long after that, Esau came in to be blessed and Isaac realized that he had made a mistake. Esau was so angry, he planned to kill his brother. Because of his coveting, Jacob had to leave home and go live with an uncle far away.

Bible Verse

"Be content with what you have, because God has said, 'Never will I leave you; never will I forsake you.'" (Hebrews 13:5b)

Instead of being greedy and wanting what other people have, we should be content in God's promise to always be with us. No matter what possessions we do or do not have, we should find contentment in God's love.

Contentment

Directions: What is the opposite of coveting? Being content with what you have. To find out what the Bible teaches about being content, <u>mark out</u> the following letters in the boxes: **B**, **F**, **J**, **K**, **Q**, and **U**. Write the leftover letters in order on the lines below the boxes. To check your work, look up 1 Timothy 6:6.

B	G	F	K	O	D	K	L
I	F	N	J	Q	E	S	F
S	W	Q	B	I	U	U	T
J	F	H	C	F	B	O	N
Q	T	K	E	U	N	T	F
M	F	E	Q	N	J	J	T
B	I	Q	S	G	F	B	R
E	J	A	K	T	G	U	K
K	A	F	B	I	J	B	N

__ __ __ __ __ __ __ __ __   __ __ __ __

__ __ __ __ __ __ __ __ __ __ __   __ __

__ __ __ __ __   __ __ __ __ __ __.

What do you think it means to be content? _____

"God Provides" Craft

God has promised to provide all your needs. He gives you that and much more! Look up 1 Timothy 6:17. Read the last part of the verse to see how generous God is with you. Remembering that He will give you what you need will help you not to covet what other people have. This craft will be a good reminder of how God cares for you.

Materials

- tissues paper of different colors
- colored markers or crayons
- Bible verse strip on this page
- green construction paper (optional)
- flower stickers
- paper or plastic cup
- green florist tape
- green pipe cleaners
- scissors
- glue
- clay

Directions

1. Cut out the Bible verse strip and glue it on the paper or plastic cup.

2. Decorate the cup with your own colorful designs and with flower stickers.

3. Cut out a 6" x 20" strip of tissue paper and fold it in half lengthwise.

4. Roll the tissue paper strip around the end of a green pipe cleaner, gathering the edges together as you roll it to make a flower.

5. Tape the bottom of the flower to the pipe cleaner with florist tape.

6. Make several flowers of different colors.*

7. Stick a glob of clay inside the cup at the bottom.

8. Stick the flower "stems" in the clay to secure them.

9. Cut a few long, thin leaf shapes from green construction paper and add them to the flowers to make an attractive bouquet.

(*Variation: Here is a way to make the flowers a bit different. Place the folded tissue paper strip on the edge of a table or desk. Scrunch the fold of the paper together a bit to crinkle it before you roll it around the pipe cleaner to make the flower.)

> See how the lilies of the field grow. They do not labor or spin. Yet, I tell you that not even Solomon in all his splendor was dressed like one of these. So do not worry. Your heavenly Father knows what you need. But seek first his kingdom and his righteousness, and all these things will be given to you as well. (Matthew 6:28–29, 31–33)

Thankfulness Finger Play

When you c-o-v-e-t

(Hold up the fingers on one hand, one by one, as you spell the word.)

What doesn't belong to you

(Point at other people.)

T-h-a-n-k the Lord

(Hold up the fingers on one hand, one by one, as you spell the word.)

For all He's given you.

(Point up toward heaven.)

Every single thing you have

(Count off on your fingers the things you have.)

Comes from God above.

(Point up toward heaven.)

Be content with what He gives

(Wag your index finger as if teaching a lesson.)

And thankful for His love.

(Put your hands over your heart.)

Culminating Activities

Help students review what they have learned about the Ten Commandments with these activities.

Signs for God's Rules

Hand out paper, pencils, and crayons or colored markers. Challenge students to create signs for all ten of God's commandments. To help them get started, place some traffic signs around the room (an octagonal stop sign, a triangular yield sign, etc.). You may want to make some rules such as "No words may be used." When everyone has finished, have students hold up their signs and explain them. Mount the signs on the wall for everyone to see.

Commands for Today Paper Chain

Materials: construction paper, scissors, glue or tape, dark colored markers

Have students cut out 20 construction paper strips about 1" wide by 9" long. Assign 10 students one each of the Ten Commandments to print on their strips. Have 10 other students (or the same 10) print the commandments in today's language on the remaining paper strips. (If time permits, discuss the Ten Commandments and let students decide together how they should be worded for easy understanding. For a shorter activity, use the "in other words" versions of the commandments at the beginning of each lesson in this book.) Then have students make loops of their paper strips and glue or tape them together in a chain. They will need to cooperate to do this. Hang the completed chain at the front of the room.

Ten Commandments Chair

This is a game for about ten children. Place chairs in a circle with the seats facing out. Begin with one less chair than children playing the game. Blow up 10 small balloons. Place a small piece of paper with a number from 1 to 10 inside each balloon before you tie it closed. Tape all 10 balloons to the back of one of the chairs. Play some music and have the children walk around the chairs as they would for a game of musical chairs. When the music stops, each child must sit in a chair. One child will not get a chair. The child who sits in the Ten Commandments chair (the balloon-decorated chair) must pop one of the balloons attached to the chair and take out the number inside. He or she must then tell the commandment for that number. Use the list below to make sure the child is right. If the child's answer is incorrect, he or she is out of the game, as is the child without a chair. However, if the child in the Ten Commandments chair answers correctly, he or she may choose someone else to leave the game. Take away a chair and start the music again. Continue until only one child is left. Make sure to leave the Ten Commandments chair in place throughout the game. Be sure to have a pin or other pointed object handy for the children to use to burst the balloons.

TEN COMMANDMENTS

1. You shall have no other gods before me.
2. Do not make idols to worship.
3. Do not misuse the name of the Lord.
4. Keep the Sabbath day holy.
5. Honor your father and mother.

6. Do not murder.
7. Do not commit adultery.
8. Do not steal.
9. Do not give false testimony.
10. Do not covet.

Before and After

Divide students into small groups. Give each group a copy of page 46. Challenge them to read the Bible verses and follow the directions to discover what God's people did before He gave them the Ten Commandments and what they did after God gave them. Let them share their findings.

Before and After

Directions: Circle the correct words to complete each sentence. Look up the Bible verses if you need help.

BEFORE

Exodus 19:1–2

1. The Israelites had been out of Egypt for
   - a. three years.
   - b. three weeks.
   - c. three months.
2. They stopped at a mountain called
   - a. Hermon.
   - b. Ranie.
   - c. Sinai.

Exodus 19:5–8

3. God promised that the Israelites would be His treasured possession if they would
   - a. obey Him fully.
   - b. go back to Egypt.
   - c. give Him a big offering.
4. The people all said
   - a. "We'll do what we want."
   - b. "We'll do everything the Lord has said."
   - c. "We'll go back to Egypt."

Exodus 19:16–18; 20:18–19

5. God came down on the mountain in thunder and lightning and
   - a. fire.
   - b. an earthquake.
   - c. hail.
6. The people were so scared by the thunder and lightning and smoke, they
   - a. ran away.
   - b. would not come close but stayed at a distance.
   - c. fainted.

AFTER

Exodus 32:1–5, 19–20

7. While Moses was up on the mountain receiving the Ten Commandments from God, the people got Aaron to
   - a. help them build a tabernacle.
   - b. go up the mountain to help Moses.
   - c. make them a golden calf idol to worship.
8. When Moses came down from the mountain and saw what the people were doing, he was so angry
   - a. he asked God to destroy them.
   - b. he threw down the commandment tablets and broke them.
   - c. he tried to kill Aaron.

Answer Key

Page 6

1. powerful
2. understanding
3. creator
4. good
5. Redeemer
6. Eternal
7. awesome
8. true
9. forgiving
10. loving
11. Lord

Page 10

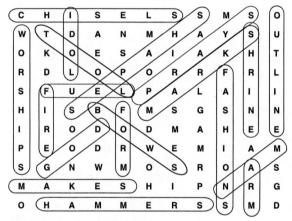

Man makes idols. God made man. Worship God!

Page 11

We know that an idol is nothing at all in the world and that there is no God but one.

Page 16

Lord, Creator, Father, Most High, Savior, Rock, Redeemer, Shepherd

Page 18

By the seventh day God had finished the <u>work</u> he had been doing; so on the seventh day he <u>rested</u> from all his <u>work</u>. And God <u>blessed</u> the seventh day and made it <u>holy,</u> because on it he <u>rested</u> from all the <u>work</u> of <u>creating</u> that he had done.

Remember that you were <u>slaves</u> in <u>Egypt</u> and that the <u>Lord</u> your God <u>brought</u> you out of there with a mighty hand and an outstretched <u>arm</u>. Therefore, the <u>Lord</u> your God has commanded you to observe the Sabbath day.

Answers will vary.

Page 19

The Sabbath was made for <u>man,</u> not <u>man</u> for the Sabbath. So the Son of Man is <u>Lord</u> even of the Sabbath.

Page 24

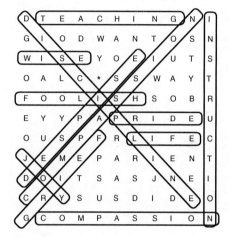

1. pride
2. compassion, compassion
3. wise, joy, foolish, grief
4. life, despise
5. discipline
6. instruction, teaching

God wants you to always obey your parents as Jesus did.

Page 26

1. Underlined: God said, 'Let us make man in our image, in our likeness—So God created man in his own image, in the image of God he created him.

2. Circled: The Lord God . . . breathed into his nostrils the breath of life—the breath of the Almighty gives me life.

3. Underlined with two lines: The Lord God formed the man from the dust of the ground.—The Spirit of God has made me.

4. Answers will vary, but should include the fact that animals were not made in God's image.

Page 27

you, be, mine, beast, plan, story
Answers will vary.

Page 30

1. F   4. C
2. B   5. A
3. E   6. D

Page 31

Page 32

2   3
1   5
4   6

Page 35

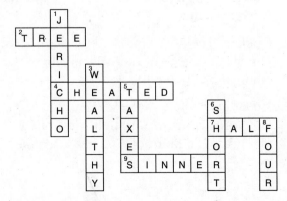

Page 36

1. Judas   3. Rachel
2. Achan   4. Jacob

Page 38

A truthful witness does not deceive, but a false witness pours out lies.

A false witness will not go unpunished, and he who pours out lies will perish.

Page 42

Godliness with contentment is great gain.
Answers will vary.

Page 46

1. c   5. a
2. c   6. b
3. a   7. c
4. b   8. b